AS MUSES BURN

MIRA HADLOW

Copyright © 2020 Miranda Williamson
All rights reserved

No part of this book may be reproduced, or stored in a retrieval system, or transmitted in any form or by any means, electronic, mechanical, photocopying, recording, or otherwise, without express written permission of the publisher.

The events portrayed in this book are probably not fictitious. Any similarity to real persons, living or dead, is not coincidental and is intended by the author.

Artwork provided by: Travis Schmiesing

PAPERBACK ISBN:	978-1-9991739-2-0
E-BOOK ISBN:	978-1-9991739-1-3
HARDCOVER ISBN:	978-1-9991739-0-6

For Dax.

Unicorns are real.

When you are old and grey and full of sleep,
And nodding by the fire, take down this book,
And slowly read, and dream of the soft look
Your eyes had once, and of their shadows deep;

How many loved your moments of glad grace,
And loved your beauty with love false or true,
But one man loved the pilgrim soul in you,
And loved the sorrows of your changing face;

And bending down beside the glowing bars,
Murmur, a little sadly, how Love fled
And paced upon the mountains overhead
And hid his face amid a crowd of stars.

W. B. Yeats - 1865-1939

OF MUSES

MIRA HADLOW

STARS

Perhaps there was a lesson in this,
waiting for bricked up windows
to become doorways,
spending days
waiting for the sun to set,
just to watch it rise again.

I traced my fingers
around silken edges
of what could be
but wasn't,
and I wondered how often
someone had counted stars
with my name
on their lips.

OF MUSES

BULLET HOLES

She never expected
to be understood.
She'd made peace with that.
She was comfortable there,
with her pockets
full of crumpled letters
she'd never send,
wearing that old jacket
with the cigarette burns
like bullet holes.

NOTHING

If you told her
she was strong,
she'd laugh
and tell you she
had nothing
left to lose.

OF MUSES

NEEDS

I was most afraid
that if our paths
should ever cross,
I would not see him,
and should I see him,
I would not know him.
and should I know him,
I would not remember
how to love him
as a man needs
to be loved.

MIRA HADLOW

MOTHER TONGUE

She put no stock in words,
but would read your pauses
like silence was her mother tongue.

ABYSS

Please

Don't ask me
to close my eyes;
there are dreams
in that darkness.

There are wishes
that will swallow
me whole
and evaporate
in the light of day.

MIRA HADLOW

MISTLETOE

I almost remember
when aloneness didn't echo,
when falling stars
granted wishes,
and mistletoe
promised kisses.

I almost recall
when gold truly glittered,
and love softly whispered.

Almost,
but then,
not at all.

OF MUSES

BRAVE

I was brave enough to fall,
but not to choose.

Strong enough to love,
but not to lose.

MIRA HADLOW

AGELESS

Where have you been,
my dearest love?

Where are you
when night turns to day
and back to night?

Where have you been
while the sun has risen and set
these thousands of times?

I've been here,
as always.
While aged beauty
became ageless
and the heaviest burdens
decayed
and became weightless.

I've been here,
on the edges of dreams and tomorrows,
collecting memories and yesterdays,
and watching each tide
bring me more
of the same.

SMALL

Please
just let me
be small
tonight.

Hide
me here
in these walls
tonight.

Come
the dawn,
I will stand
and fight,
but please
just let me
fall
tonight.

MIRA HADLOW

GENTLE SOUL

You terrify me, gentle soul.
When you stand guard.
When you stand strong.
When you stand down.

When you meet
the tides
of my anguish
with patient grace.

When you pick up
the pieces of my frailty
and hand my strength
back to me.

When you bear witness
to reluctant words.
Or wishes.
Or silence.

You terrify me, gentle soul,
when you inspire me
to dream,
or believe,
or want to begin again.

OF MUSES

NAME IT

I told myself I hadn't seen it.
I called it by a hundred other names.

To name it was to know,
to know was to feel,
to feel was to hope,
and hope was bound
with barbed strands
of cynicism
most days.

MIRA HADLOW

RESTLESS

She would look you dead in the eye
and tell you she was a restless soul.
She had simply forgotten
how to stop running
from how much he felt like home.

MORTALITY

I avoided falling in love wherever possible,
not because I was filled with fear
over the possibility of loss,
but in solemn acknowledgment
of my own mortality,
dread, over the inevitability of it.

MIRA HADLOW

ESCAPE

Just to escape
sometimes.
Just to be free
sometimes.

To be careless
or hopeless
or weightless
or reckless-
or maybe
just painless,
but only just
sometimes.

FREE

She wanted little,
expected less,
and needed more
than she knew of.

She'd laugh
and flick her cigarette
if you tried to give her
anything at all,

and she'd tell you
that anything free
was more
than she could afford.

MIRA HADLOW

CHAOS

If, when you kiss me,
my lips taste only of chaos,
please,
don't
kiss me

twice.

OF MUSES

KEEPSAKE

It was the most peculiar thing.
Her treasured box of keepsakes
was only just a box of 'almost'.

MIRA HADLOW

RISK

I walked away.
I wrapped cynicism
around the broken pieces
that dared me to hope,
and I walked away
before I remembered
how to dream.

SIREN

Her longing rose
and fell
with timeless tides.

She beckoned the brave
and foolhardy alike,
and would drown either
on a whim without mercy,
simply because the moon
refused to set sail.

FARTHER

Do you see behind silent eyes
can you tell truth from lies?
Serpentine statements,
lowered gazes;
tongue in cheek,
hypnotic phrases.
You'll only see what you will;
I'll pull you in,
but farther still.

OF MUSES

MELANCHOLY

In the absence of a lover,
I was satisfied to make love
to my own melancholy.

LIAR

I tried
to be brave
or ferocious
or fearless,
but my heart
had a softness
that bled
too easily
and it made
a liar of me.

ART

She was some
precarious balance
of shadow and light.

Because those who feel
the weight of beauty
always risk
being destroyed by it.

She was madness,
but she was art.

PLATITUDES

It was days like this.
Days when words
threatened to fall
from the sky,
or when they rose
and hardened in my throat.

Days when the untold,
unsaid things
rose to the surface,
and nearly bubbled
over the edge.
Days when repression and rage
blistered my tongue.
It was days like this
that I offered you platitudes.

REPRIEVE

No need have I
for a love that bellows,
that shakes the earth
or churns the skies.
My voice quakes
with ancient echoes
and my heaving chest
commands the seas.

Nor have I want
for breathless passion,
I long for a love
that will hide me from these.
Teach me of peace,
teach me to breathe,
be my reprieve.

LONGING

If ever he were mine,
I'd have nothing left in
this world.

OF MUSES

REQUIRE

I told him to love me
from the other side
of the world,
and I told my fear
that longing
was required
of art.

MIRA HADLOW

THIS WAY

I will love you this way.

I will love you
in empty palms,
and airless words,
and wanting
for something
to want for.

I will love you
in the longing,
and never
risk the loss.

PERHAPS

Perhaps
we were
too different.

Or worse.

Perhaps
we'd feed
each other's demons
and end up somewhere
on the south side of hell.

Perhaps
we'd find healing,
and passion,
and we'd shift
the earth
on its axis.

Which might be
the most terrifying
outcome of all.

MIRA HADLOW

FIX

Please don't do this,
because you fix things,
and I'm broken.

Because you fix things
to avoid the discomfort
of loving them.

Because when you fix me,
you'll be uncomfortable
with loving me,
and I'll have to
walk away.

OF MUSES

BEAUTIFUL

She was beautiful, to be sure.

She was beautiful in her tragedy.
In the way her eyes were haunted
by some unspoken thing.
In the way she paused sometimes,
or let silence
speak in her stead.

She was beautiful in her madness.
In her jumbled thoughts,
and the way she talked too fast.
Or too much.

In the way she laughed
at jokes she hadn't yet told,
and giggled at nothing at all.

MIRA HADLOW

She was beautiful in her chaos.
In her wild ideas,
and the way her heart broke and bled
for a hundred different strangers
and never for herself.

She was beautiful in her frailty.
In the way she was fearless.
Or ferocious.
Or uncomfortable
with being fought for.

In the way she'd rather speak
of the beauty in you.

WHAT IF

I had been here before,
on the edge of what if.

I knew what it was to leap,
or turn back,
and I knew what it was
to fall.

I wrapped my fists
around cut-and-run,
and asked
if you were the one
I'd run to
or run from.

DESTROY

If I asked you
to come here
and destroy me,
we both know
that you
couldn't
or wouldn't
out of fear
of healing
us both.

OF MUSES

EXCEPT

She could walk away
from anything or anyone,
if it no longer served her.

Except from hope.

Even the hope of finding hope
buried barbs in her veins,
and she'd happily stay
and bleed to death.

MIRA HADLOW

I KNOW

I wondered sometimes,
what we would say
if ever our lives
weren't in the way.

I wondered if words
would be enough,
or if they'd fall flat.

Or be needed at all.

I wondered sometimes,
if silence would reign,
and if the unspoken things
would fall at the feet
of "I know".

OF MUSES

TALES

Speak to me
in words unspoken
of distant seas
and hearts unbroken,
of anguished pauses
and broken lines,
unspoken clauses
and halted time;
of vows we kept
in other lives
or tears we wept,
or just of mine.

BRACING

And there it was again.
The fear.
Bracing for impact,
for silence,
for cold.

Drowning.
Swells of panic,
salty skin,
cut-and-run.

I could never tell
if I was more afraid
of the harbor
or the storm.

PALMISTRY

I knew that I had known him before,
in some distant time and place,
as if the lines on our palms
were maps to each other.

KEEP

She wasn't the kind of girl you chased.
She couldn't be claimed
or caught
or won.
She couldn't be bought,
and she wasn't
the kind of girl that stayed.

She would strip your soul naked,
and become
whatever you needed.

The only way to keep her
was by needing
nothing at all.

OF MUSES

PRETEND

He spoke of his disdain
for matters of the heart
while speaking freely
of mine.

We both pretended
that I couldn't see
the softness in his soul,
as if strength
and longing
negated each other.

STRINGS

So I wound words
around wishes,
like strings
around fingers,
and dared you to find me
behind shrouded eyes
and wee hours
confessions.

I left my laughter
to echo in hallways,
and prayed
that somehow
you'd find me
in dreams.

ALCHEMY

But I saw it.
Edges of brokenness glittered,
and shards reflected silver,
as strands of light and joy.

I saw the sorrow
and the little pieces of himself
he'd tucked under corners.

I saw mosaics of light,
and shadows,
and the alchemy
of creating love from nothing.

And he was beautiful.

POCKETS

I tried to imagine
what he was like
as a child.

Soft hearted.
Misunderstood,
I guessed.

Wild hair,
wilder ideas
and pockets
full of treasures;
reminders
of who he aspired to be.

I supposed
that not much
had changed.

ENOUGH

I'd find him there sometimes,
just sitting,
staring at the horizon.

Wondering
if he would be a better man,
or different, somehow.

Stronger, perhaps,
or braver, maybe.

Or enough.
Maybe just enough.

MIRA HADLOW

SEE

His words spoke of more
than anything he ever said.
I wished he could see
how brokenness
made him brave,
how compassion
made him strong,
how his longing to lay down roots
gave him wings,
and I wished he could see
how I loved him.

OF MUSES

BREAK

Please, lover.
break my heart.
Broken open,
into pieces,
past defenses
and my reasons.
Shatter anguish,
latent rage;
past the stronghold,
terror's cage.
Please, lover.
break my heart.

MIRA HADLOW

PROMISES

Promises of forever fall on deaf ears, lover.
You need not let good intentions make a liar of you.
Promise me that you will be kind.
Promise me that you will speak truth.
Promise me that you will be brave.

MAYBE

Speak to me of maybes,
and maybe I'll tell you of mine.
But maybe I know that wishes fall flat
the moment you give them a name,
and maybe I need us to stay.

IMMUNE

He asked questions
and spoke in riddles,
as if being an enigma
would make him immune
to falling in love.

OF MUSES

SCARS

I want to know your scars,
if they bled and if they still do.
I want to know why you cringe
at honeyed words that
fall from my lips.

I want your pain.
Your love.
Your laughter.

I want to know if she touched your face
before she broke your heart,
and if you shattered a thousand times
when you walked away.

I want to hear your voice
beyond the resonance
that drowns
the beating of your heart.

I need to taste the words on your lips,
and know the why,
and the how,
and wonder
what they mean.

MIRA HADLOW

HOPE

I curled my aching fingers
around fistfuls of maybe,
and called it hope.

OF MUSES

TEMPEST

We built sandcastles sometimes,
on some imaginary shoreline,
building cities from seashells
and sun kissed wishes.

We would taunt the tide
and laugh as waves crashed
over kingdoms,
or we'd sigh as the sea
claimed our dreams as its own.

We raced tides sometimes,
through make-believe caverns,
filling rocky rooms
with untold stories
just to hear the caves tell
our tales back to us.

We'd run our hands along walls
and sit in reverent awe
when we happened upon chambers
we were certain
that no one else
had ever seen.

We braved squalls sometimes,
in some fantastical ocean,
daring tempests
to drag us
to salty depths,
and refusing
to loosen our hold
on each other.

I'd become part of this,
of this vastness,
and it of me.

I'd rather drown here,
than walk on land alone.

BRAZEN

He was brazen.
Brave.
Unmoved by dissention,
but I could tell
that the softness
in his soul
caused him some conflict.

He was hungry.
For truth.
For love.
For life.
For home.

MAP

I traced the lines
on his palms
like a map
that could lead me
to somewhere
I didn't have
to run from.

RAIN

You heard the thunder in me,
and told me you loved the rain.

I supposed perhaps you did,
and I supposed perhaps
the rain and I
were meant to be loved
in the same way.

From a distance,
from shelter,
and only sometimes.

MIRA HADLOW

FRAGMENTS

You only gave me
pieces of you.

Fragments.

Treasures pulled
from denim pockets,
with bits of string
and crumpled paper
and an old grocery list.

I held them
close to my heart,
and I knew
they were all
you had to give.

DROWN

There was an intoxicating
sort of madness
in the way his lips
tasted like surrender,
and his voice
seemed to call
the tides to the shore.

In the way
he could push
and pull
at the same time.

I wanted nothing
but to drown.

MIRA HADLOW

PUDDLES

Somewhere between
muddy hands
and carving our initials
into puddles,
I realized
there is only
what we do now,
and what we do next.

HEAR

He asked
if I could carry his laughter
as I carried his sorrow,
or hear his joy
as I heard his anguish.

He asked
if maybe
that could
be enough.

MIRA HADLOW

DEFEAT

And so we raged,
or we danced,
or we wept
in joyous defeat
of each other's misery,
but mostly we clasped hands
that were just out of reach.

MERCY

I could not offer you salvation,
or redemption,
or even reprieve,
but perhaps,
in some silent lullaby,
I could offer you mercy.

MIRA HADLOW

FRAILTY

I stood there,
both fists clenched
around the lump in my throat,
eyes full of cut-and-run.

You built fences around
the scorched earth
at my feet,
and stood guard
while I spoke
to my frailty.

LAYOVER

He was waiting to catch a plane.

I was helping him pass the time
and he was saving me
from the depths of hell.

He wanted to know
what burned my soul
deepest and widest.

I should have asked him
If he'd like to try.

BLOODLETTING

We found ourselves,
bloodletting in ambrosial dawn.

In those hours, when silent things
are spoken
or sung,
in languages
we may never learn.

Just souls.

Drifting.
Limbless.
Or weightless
for a time.

He held a torch in one hand,
and a mirror in the other,
and he bared his throat briefly,
before the day
spoke the truth.

OF MUSES

LADY LUCK

"Yeah. Lady Luck.
But not 'cause you're lucky,
and we both know
you ain't no lady."

Cigarette smoke played coy,
curling around the corners
of your sharpened grin.

"Lady luck.
Because this is gonna
cost me everything,
and the only thing
I'll be sore about
is not having more
to lose."

MIRA HADLOW

LOOK

I've looked for you
in everyone I've
ever loved.

ECHO

We shared a common emptiness.
Not necessarily a sadness,
and certainly not a wound,
and neither
felt an urgency
to repair it,
or heal it,
or fill it
with anything.

An emptiness.

Some shapeless, nameless,
hollow spot in our souls.

We both met it
with a melancholy
sort of pragmatism,
and perhaps
an understanding
that certain things
were meant to echo.

MIRA HADLOW

TASTE

I can't help myself.
His lips taste like hope,
girlish dreams,
and heartache.

OF MUSES

REDEMPTION

You told me that my lips tasted like rage,
and I wondered if that was just another word
for redemption.

MIRA HADLOW

MISUNDERSTOOD

Here we are.
So close to heaven.
Or hell.
Or nothing.

Where unseen and unsaid
need no explanation.

Where hope and sorrow fall away,
in pursuit of something greater.

 Or wiser.
Or maybe:
just less misunderstood.

OF MUSES

REST

Rest, my darling.
Pour your tears
on my outstretched hands,
and begin again.

MIRA HADLOW

DESTROY ME

I knew your soul by the way
you spoke to mine.
I knew your longing.
Your power.
Your pain.

I knew you could destroy me
like no one ever had.
And I knew
I'd let you.

OF MUSES

UNDERSTOOD

Suddenly, he made sense to me.
His longing.
his need to be better,
be stronger,
be more.

How he'd retreat and create things,
as if he could change the world
by pulling away from it.

And I wondered
who made him believe
that he wasn't enough.

MIRA HADLOW

FOREVERMORE

Can you reach beyond the silence,
beyond the blackness
of the darkest night?

Can you speak so I can hear you,
silent words that softly
touch my soul?

Can you see behind the mirror,
past reflected truths
and lies alike?

In that place,
that secret chamber,
I'll wait for you
forevermore.

OF MUSES

SAVE YOU

I can't save you,
but I can see you.
and maybe that's enough.

MIRA HADLOW

EDEN

And if there was a God,
I wondered
if we'd been made
to share a soul,
or if my chest
contained a rib
he'd stolen
from you.

AMIDST STARS

We hide here sometimes,
amidst stars.

Here, in this in this kingdom
we built just for us.

Here, in this place,
where hope hovers weightless,
and truth rises shameless,
and fear somehow weighs less -
and love asks for nothing
but the space to breathe.

Sometimes we dine with our demons;
not as foes,
but as scholars,
and ask them
what they mean to teach us.

MIRA HADLOW

Sometimes I speak to yours,
or you to mine,
and sometimes
we stand guard for each other.

We make grand plans,
and speak of far off places,
and distant lands
we'll likely never see.

We hide - in this -
where elephants stalk corridors,
and we brace against dreams
or the dawn
that will steal us away.

OF MUSES

MAGAZINES

He spoke
of his heart
like a place
he had only seen
in magazines.

MIRA HADLOW

BRIGHTER DAYS

I told him
that he couldn't save me
from my chosen darkness,
and that better men
had failed on
brighter days.

OF MUSES

DRUNK

We always came back to this place,
deaf to the other's silver tongue,
intrigued by the notion
of being disarmed.

And here,
immune to the lyrical elixirs
that intoxicated those
who wouldn't see us,
perhaps we could fill
the silence with truth.

SKIN

My skin smelled like you
and I wondered
how long it had been
since I'd been kissed
by someone
whose lips
tasted like maybe -the way
you kissed me
this morning.

OF MUSES

VICE

I asked you
to name your vice,
your drug of choice.

We both
pretended
it wasn't me.

MIRA HADLOW

LET ME BE

When your soul is weary,
and your heart is heavy,
let me be.

When worry and sorrow
draw lines on your brow,
let me be.

When laughter crinkles your eyes,
and joy turns your face to the sky,
let me be.

Let me be present.
Let me be witness.
Let me be her.

OF MUSES

EARTH AND SEA

I never knew
which of us
was the tide,
and which
was the shore,
but we called to
and collided with
one another,
retreated
just as certainly,
and took something with us
each time.

AVATARS

There was a beauty in this,
in this madness,
this place where we lived other lives.

We took other lovers,
and broke other hearts,
and sometimes our own.

We built fences
around patches of scorched earth
and called them gardens,
or built empires
that made us forget
we were alone.

We moved like avatars
through this life,
and retreated into each other
when we needed to remember
what it felt like to breathe.

CATCH

I don't believe
You'd have come here
if you'd known
I would fall.

Or if you'd known
that you'd catch me.

Or that I'd catch you too.

MIRA HADLOW

ALL OF IT

Well, here it is.
All of it.

Some of it's in pieces;
it's not in any sort of order.

It's not whole,
or presentable,
and it's not all pretty.

I've collected all the hidden bits;
the fragments of shame
hidden away,
swept into corners out of sight,
and the dreams
too fragile for the light.

It's not all pretty,
but it's all have.
and I'd like to show you.

THERE

I'll see you there.
Where things don't get lost
between what
and what now.

I'll see you
in that life
where words don't hang airless
and stop midflight.

I'll see you
in that place
where dreams and not fears
grow roots and flourish,
and refuse to drown
in love's downpour.

MIRA HADLOW

OUTSKIRTS

I was never yours,
nor you mine,
but somehow
we belonged to each other.

I was never sure
if I called you to my dreams
or was beckoned to yours,
but we met there sometimes,
on the outskirts of never,
where today shared a border
with someday.

For moments in time,
we were free.

Elephants didn't
stalk corners of bedrooms,
and unsaid things
weren't as heavy
somehow.

POISONED FRUIT

Let the lies
fall from your lips
and take root
in my soul.

I'll not concern myself
with the poisoned fruit.

ANYWAY

I loved you anyway.

I loved you
on days
when you were distracted
by making partners
of pastimes.

I loved you
in hours
that floated in limbo,
unclaimed by both
yesterday and tomorrow.

I loved you
on nights
when your hunger
beckoned me to dreams
that felt like declarations.

I loved you
with abandon,
without condition,
beyond reason,
anyway.

OF MUSES

EDGES

It had always been this way.

We flitted around the edges
of each other's lives,
understanding too much
and too little,
the way lovers are prone to do.

We made love with our minds,
with our words.
with our souls.

Sometimes gently, tenderly
or with wild abandon,
clawing at thresholds,
pushing deeper,
in perfect rhythm,
and over the edge.

We gave our all
and nothing
at the same time,
covering our nakedness
as quickly as we exposed it,
and we vanished again
until the next time we didn't.

TELL ME

Tell me
what you believe in,
what you run from,
and what you crave.

Tell me
what moves your soul
like ancient muses,
and what song
owns the flesh
and bones of you.

Tell me
what wraps itself
around your rage,
or shackles you
to sorrow.

Tell me
what you long for,
that I might stop
the rain.

RIBBONS

I stood there,
not unlike some feeble straw shanty,
constructed on some shoreline,
begging the wind
and the sea to spare it.

And somehow,
your words reached into my heart
and embroidered themselves there.

Sentences,
like alchemy,
strands of gold.

Strands became ribbons,
until ribbons
became rooftops.

And somehow,
I was something greater.

Something grander,
with hallways
and pillars of gold,
and the sea
and the wind
at my feet.

MIRA HADLOW

JOY

Dream with me.
Dream of lazy days,
frosty nights just for us,
and kisses
that taste
like hot cocoa
and joy.

Dream of belonging
somewhere.
Here,
to each other.

Dream of watching
ten thousand
shared tomorrows
become yesterdays,
and how
that would be
a dream
come true.

SLEEP

To rest,
or fall silent,
or asleep.

Here,
where gardens
disguise shackled demons,
where ruins shroud innocence,
and seasons change
with lowered lashes
and glimmers of hope.

Here,
where shrapnel
is scattered,
from shanties
built at low tide.

Where sirens sing
haunted lullabies
to empty shorelines.

Where potted thistles
are watered
and called gardens,
and sleep has evaded
heavy eyes and heavy souls
for a thousand years.

Here,
where the darkest of these
holds the storm,
and the wolf
stands guard for the lamb.

OF MUSES

HER NAME

He spoke her name
in reverent awe,
as some sacred hymn;
or ancient incantation,
reserved for the only
the most righteous
of men.

He spoke her name
the way condemned men
speak of mercy,
and the dying
speak of lives
well lived.

He spoke her name
as soldiers
speak of a queen
worth dying for,
and holy men
speak of their gods.

He spoke the name
of his raven-haired queen;
he held it on his tongue
as a sacred sacrament,
and I was sure
I was not worthy
of ever speaking
her name.

MIRA HADLOW

HOME

I will speak your name
in softest whispers
when your heavy soul
requires a balm.

I will sing to you
in sacred lullabies,
and put to shame
the siren's song

I will call your name
from distant shorelines,
should your compass
lead you wrong

I will speak to you
in incantations
and show the King
which way is home.

OFFERING

I wished
for something
to give you.

A token of love,
or a ribbon,
or a lock of hair,
or anything
that wasn't
already yours.

MIRA HADLOW

HONEY

The words drifted so easily
from your lips.
Like laughter.
Like honey.

You told me you loved me
so effortlessly.

I thought maybe sincerity
demanded some angst;
but I supposed
that I felt at home,
and I supposed
that I loved you too.

FIND ME

You would find me.
Here.

If yesterday crumbled
and the world fell away,
you would find me.
Unmoved.

If the air was heavy
with the ashes
of their gods,
you would find me.
Unbroken.

If my hands were all
that could heal you.

And if I was swept
into some darkness,
greater than me,
greater than this,
you would find me
then too.

LEGEND

Immortality is achieved
by igniting the heart
and soul of a writer.

Make me love you,
and I'll make you a legend.

OF MUSES

TIME

Love me
like you're running
out of time.

MIRA HADLOW

SUNDAYS

White linens
and my head on your chest,
watching dust sparkle
through lazy Sunday sunbeams
streaming through windows.

We'll watch the seasons change,
and hair turn grey,
while the coffee brews
on Sunday mornings.

DAISY

He stood there,
grinning as if
he'd brought me a daisy,
instead of holding
the moon on a string.

MIRA HADLOW

MAGIC

He was magic.

He had a quiet knowingness
that perfection
was found in the broken bits,
that beauty
demanded nothing
but the space to exist,
and that gentleness
needed no explanation.

OF MUSES

BUILD

You were born to build,
my love,
but not to build
things as trivial
as what can be held
on your hands.

You were born to
build kingdoms.

MIRA HADLOW

LIFETIMES

I could love you
for a thousand lifetimes,
and still not
have loved you
enough.

OF MUSES

TIME

I met a man
who told me
he loved me.

I supposed
that he'd loved
other things,
in other times,
as I'd been loved
by other men,
living other lives.

But for a moment,
this man, and I
found peace in words
now etched in time.

MIRA HADLOW

DRAGON

We hunted dreams
by candlelight,
or by the light of the moon.

We spoke in near darkness
of who we'd become
in the light of day,
and we chased hope
like a dragon.

OF MUSES

PLEDGE

We pledged ourselves
to our own morality
as we understood it;
we married ourselves
to the righting of wrongs
and the solitary quest to understand,
to achieve,
to awaken.

We told ourselves
that we found freedom there,
and indeed we did.

We found freedom from ideology,
from oppression,
from the blindness of doctrine,
and our knees never touched soil
in the name of any man or god.

We freed ourselves
from being understood,
from being shackled
to any fictional sense of belonging,
but mostly,
we freed ourselves
from knowing what it was
to be loved.

MIRA HADLOW

STAND

It is there,
in the silent
resonance of
"I will stand with you",
that love exists
in its purest form.

LEAN

Lean into me deeply.
Let me give you reprieve
from your demons,
and me from mine.

MIRA HADLOW

THORNS

I wore your tears in my hair
like a diamond studded
crown of thorns.

OF MUSES

MODEL

Two thousand photographs.
Moments in time
when I was your muse.

Suspended.
Airless.

Motionless laughter
and frozen echoes in alleyways,
and stairwells that time forgot.

Wind tousled hair, train tracks,
and eyes brimming with tears
that will never fall.

I still wonder what you saw.
Or who she was.

Why she was magic,
and madness,
and why she looked like me.

MIRA HADLOW

SAFE
He was
the safest
place I'd
ever been.

GO

Don't speak.

Just hold my hand
in this soundless place,
because silence
lends a knowingness
that asks nothing of us,
and words leave too much room
for misunderstanding.

Just sit with me.
Here.

Do away with
the mundane things
we'd speak of
if we had nothing
to say at all.

Because if we speak
of the mundane things,
one of us will eventually say
it's time to go.

MAGDALENE

I wondered if
he could walk
on water,
so I poured
my tears
on his feet.

OF MUSES

THIS

This place.
Where I can hear
despite the silence.

Where we are defined
by who we are
and who we aspire to be,
and not by the choices
we've made.

Where why
has more weight than what,
and weary souls
find refuge in being known.

This place.

Where time ebbs and flows
through unspoken things
that finally get said.

MIRA HADLOW

Where the fear of want
and wanting more
has no power.

Where mosaiced minds
Transition seamlessly in lockstep,
and longing has nothing to long for,
for a time.

Hide me here.

In this.

SOUNDLESS

Let me show you the power of silence.
Sit with me in this soundless place.
Look.
Fix your gaze.
Beyond my eyes, and mine beyond yours.

MIRA HADLOW

UNMOVED

I see you, as always, as ever.
When you are strong,
or when your grief
burns hot against your flesh.

When you have stood unmoved
by the tides of my anguish,
and when ten thousand sorrows
have brought you to your knees.

When I have pounded
my grief into your chest,
my fists clenched
around silent rage,
and when you have poured
your sorrow on my feet.

OF MUSES

FRIDAY

I will not be your Friday night
or your Tuesday afternoon,
I will not be your secret,
your pastime, or your muse.
I will not be your Madonna,
your angel, or your whore
I will not be your addiction,
your affliction, your salvation,
or your cure.
But only as your Queen,
all of these and more.

NOVEMBER

Three in the morning,
in the cold of November,
you stood in my doorway,
with your hat in your hands.

You called me brave,
and ferocious, and fearless,
and you spoke of a softness
so few understand.

Three in the morning,
words spoken in earnest
turning wishes to pledges
and doubt into hope.

You promised to love me
better than muses and maybes,
and I thought you deserved
to come in from the cold.

OF MUSES

AGAINST

And when my eyes finally closed
against the day,
against the grief.

Heavy.
Sedated.
Defeated.

You found me there.
You found me in that place,
where your storms
pulled ancient trees from the ground,
where weary bones begged
for somewhere to fall.

You found me in that place,
where rooms were too small,
and time went in circles.

Or stood still.

And you begged me
to show you
how to close your eyes
against it all.

MIRA HADLOW

QUIET

I will love you in the quiet,
in the spaces between
the moments that define us.
In the silence between words
thought but not spoken,
and when time stands still,
as today becomes tomorrow.

I will love you in the silence
of knowing looks,
of clasped hands,
and the steam of hot coffee.

In the split second
when inhaling
becomes exhaling.

And when this life is over,
and our bodies become ash,
I will love you
in the silence
of forever.

ALWAYS

It had always been you.
On days when joy
fluttered unburdened
and on days
when sorrow
longed for somewhere
to fall.

Somewhere in years
of clasped hands,
and hearts,
and whispered daydreams,
and fears,
we learned how to love and be loved,
but mostly,
we taught
each other
to risk it all.

DREAMS

I'll meet you there,
where sequined secrets
in far off places
tell tales of what
you do not say.

Where sultry blues float
from ivory keys,
and you pull me close
just to tell me to stand.

In that place
between who we've been
and who we'll be.
Or who we won't.

I'll meet you there.
In dreams.

FLY

I know that kind of love.
The kind that breaks down
everything you thought you knew
and builds something better.

The kind that demands
you set yourself on fire
and lay at its feet.

The kind that consumes,
and heals,
and grows,
and expands,
for no reason
other than to exist.

The kind of love
that will teach you to fly.

MIRA HADLOW

SIT

You and I will never change.
If you need to rage,
I'll rage with you.
If you need to weep,
I'll help turn streams to rivers.
If you need to sit,
I have silence to share.
If you don't know what you need,
I'll sit with you
in your unknowingness
until you either know,
or don't need.

OF MUSES

SPOKE

But sometimes
with too much to say,
or too little.
We spoke in stops.
Or starts.
Or not at all.

MIRA HADLOW

NIGHT

We wrapped ourselves
in the safety of the wee hours.

Baring hearts,
baring souls,
baring throats.

The night seemed to nod
as if she promised
to keep our secrets
from the light of day.

SACRED

Oh, but I loved you,
But not in a way
that demanded
a single thing.

I loved you purely.
In recognition.
In appreciation.
I loved you
like sacred things
are meant
to be loved.

MIRA HADLOW

BECAUSE

Because you stay.
because you are not moved
when I burn too hot
or too bright.
because you are not fooled
when I dare the gods
or wage war.
because you walk headlong
into the teeth of my sorrow,
and you stay.

OF MUSES

BROKEN ARROWS

Bring me
your broken arrows,
and aching palms.

Bring me your war,
and the violence
at the corners
of your mouth.

Bring me your need
for peace.
For reprieve.

Bring me your anguish,
that I might braid it
into my hair,
that you might rest,
or find peace,
when the day burns hot,
and when it sleeps.

MIRA HADLOW

THUNDER

And somehow,
the thunder in him
silenced the thunder in me.

FALL

You can take your time, my love.
There are no demands tonight, my love.
The world can wait outside, my love.

Let the world
slow
down.

Let me show you peace, my love.
For a moment - just be, my love.
Pour your sorrow at my feet, my love.

If you need to fall,
fall
down.

MIRA HADLOW

UNWIND
Unwind me.
As you do.

OF MUSES

PRAY

I could taste heaven
on your mouth
and see God in your eyes.

I wasn't sure
if I sought redemption,
or to be pulled
to my knees
and taught
how to pray.

SHAMELESS

Somewhere.
You were here.
Or I was there.

I heard voices
in four part harmony,
and distant chords
in a minor key.

We were breathless.
And shameless.
And weightless.
And blameless.

And for a moment,
I had all of you,
and you of me.

OF MUSES

ALL

I want you inside my body
as deeply
as you penetrated my mind.
My heart.
My soul.

Wrap your hands
around my hips.

Don't let go.

Make me scream.
Make me pray.
Make me run.
Make me stay.

I will take all of you,
and nothing less.

SIN

There were nights sometimes.
Nights when you owned me.
Nights at your mercy.

Clawing at silence,
begging for freedom,
but praying for none.

And you.
All composure
and mischief,
writing our secrets
on my thighs
in words that tasted
like surrender
and sin.

OF MUSES

TONGUES

Lick your name
from my lips
like honey,
like holy wine,
and make
me speak
in tongues.

UNDRESS

Trace your hands down my spine
and unlace the steel boned decorum
that binds me to everything
outside this room.

Breathe deeply into my neck;
lay claim to what
has been yours all along.

Pull my hips to yours,
give me your all.

Be you saint or savage,
victor or villain,
push into me deeply;
you've found your way home.

PENANCE

Biding time.
As always, as ever.
In my silence.
Knowing now, speaking never.
Wasted lines
taste of blood, taste of lust.
No more penance.
I'll fuck you with my words at last.

MIRA HADLOW

TRY

I need you
to want
to drown in me,
and then
need you
to try.

STAY

Indulge.
At your pleasure,
at your mercy,
you at mine.

Lust.
licked from
hungry fingers,
or running slick
under my thighs.

Claim.
Take more
of what is yours,
until there's nothing
left to take.

My body
is your home.

Stay.

AWAKE

Awake.
Silent and starving
for calloused hands
and stuttered sighs,
and the taste of longing
on hungry tongues
when words no longer serve us.

Awake.
Breathless and craving
for decorum unlaced.
Unraveled. Unbound.
For the savagery
in your indulgence.

Awake.
Longing and praying
to see you standing
at my door
and that you'll take
all that you came for.

OF MUSES

FUCK ME

He looked at me
like he understood
my particular
brand of rage.

I told him to fuck me
so I could feel anything
but that.

MIRA HADLOW

WORSHIP

I didn't want
for much, but
the gnashing of teeth,
the baring of souls,
and to worship
at the feet
of each other's
pleasure.

OF MUSES

INCANTATION

He spoke my name
like an incantation,
and I wanted to lick
the words
from his lips

OF ASHES

MISTRESS

You arrived without warning
-as always-
with blistered palms,
in those coldest, oldest days,
seeking a warmth
you had come to expect.

Sometimes I stripped naked
and danced for you,
or sometimes
I showed you my body.

We clasped hands and hearts,
and bared souls or throats,
and pledged fealty to the truth.

We drew blood
with the things we spoke of,
and danced until dawn
around the things we didn't,
and got drunk
on asking nothing at all.

There were many secrets in that place;
things I'd never say
or never hear,
but I knew
that your secret
was me.

OF MUSES

MERCILESS

If we had met
sometime
between then and now,
and then again,
I wondered
if we loved
each other mercilessly,
If I could hear you then,
and you could see me.

FAITH

I stitched my lies
to my flesh,
and for a moment
I had something
to believe in.

OF MUSES

DINNER

She won't stay here.
Not forever.
Here on the outskirts of maybe,
where love tastes strangely
like silence
and dinner for one.

OF ASHES

SCRIPTED

Every word you spoke,
like ink on my skin.
scripted stories,
spoken on a thousand
other empty nights,
to other hungry souls.
and I needed
to be somewhere
other than here.

or to breathe.
or to burn.
or to drown.

CRIMSON

Forgive me.
You loved me better
when I lied.
You pulled me closer,
kissed me more deeply,
as if fallacies
stained my lips
a shade of red
you couldn't resist.

Forgive me
if I bloodied my tongue
to give you
the shade of crimson
you craved.

MADNESS

We called our madness
by other names
in order to make it palatable.

We called it passion,
except on the days
it soured
and caught
in our throats.

On those days,
we called it love.

OF MUSES

CLAIM

I have lived
a hundred lifetimes
and known a thousand men.
You're man enough
to speak your mind,
but too cowardly to claim me.

OF ASHES

LOST

This was the cruelest of ironies;
you only loved the parts of me
that needed finding,
and I had to choose
between losing everything,
and staying lost.

OF MUSES

ON FIRE

My love
can set your soul on fire,
or it can burn your world
to the ground.

FORFEIT

I wasn't sure
when she decided
that longing
was required of love,
but there was
a day in June,
when hollow hallways
weren't enough.

There was a day
when the sun rose
on her tomorrows,
and adoration unrequited
slept at the feet
of goodbye.

OF MUSES

FLY

Please,
if you are kind:
if you are kind,
you must be cruel.
You must make her
leave this place.
and not return to you.

If you let her love you,
she'd forget to fly,
and clip her own wings.
If she thought
she could heal you,
she'd bleed to death
at your feet.

EPITAPH

I wrote your name, sometimes.
On fogged up windows, or on paper,
on my palms, as if I could touch you.
on my thighs, as if you could live there.
uncertain if your name
was more epitaph or prose.

OF MUSES

GONE

And then again. There it was.
After years
of learning to live sleepless
as a way
of vanquishing dreams
that never came true.
After needs unmet,
dreams undreamed,
and tears unshed.

There it was.

Airless, defenseless,
suspended in slow motion.

Broken, bleeding,
wanting and needing
to love and be loved,
to save and be saved,
to see and be seen.

Shaken awake.
Shaken alive.
There it was.
And gone again.

OF ASHES

INFERNO

That's the trouble with having fire
in your soul.

It always needs something to burn.

OF MUSES

FADE

This too will fade.
In time.

Darkness becomes
ambrosial dawn,
then light of day
and back to night.

This - will pass
as you and I.
In time.

Seasons grow
weary and sleep.
What ifs become what was
or wasn't.

And all becomes
the stuff of legend.

Or not.
In time.

COULD

I could have loved you
better.
Longer, perhaps.

I could have loved you
in sunburnt smiles,
and muddy palms,
and roads to nowhere,
or roads to home.

I could have loved you
in old houses,
and string lights in cedars,
and shared daydreams,
or shared nights.

I could have loved you
better,
longer,
or forever,
had I not needed
to be loved in return.

OF MUSES

NIGHTCAP

Your tears sank into my hair;
you spoke of love unending.

I shared my body,
I shared my bed,
and you told her
you loved her
this morning.

TEPID

I will leave you as I left them;
those who were enthralled,
or amused,
but refused
to wear claw marks
on the insides
of their soul.

Those who were distracted,
or even addicted,
but uncomfortable
with leaving the shore.

Those who would name me,
but not claim me,
and those who tried to drink
and not be dragged under.

Perhaps someday
you'll hear my siren song
from the tepid waters
of the shoreline,
and wish
you'd chosen
to drown.

LAUNDRY

You mocked
at my palms full of hope.

Problematic.
Or chaotic.

When I stayed up all night
to see the sun,
or found hope
where there was none.

You sneered
at my clothes on the floor.

Dirty.
Or discarded.

As if you hadn't torn them
from me yourself,
and I wanted to lay
my flesh beside them
for the same reasons.

OF ASHES

HELL

He looked at me
like maybe
I could heal him,
as if I could
relieve his anguish
simply by seeing it.

I knew he would follow me
if I asked him to,
but he needed
to find his way home,
and I was going
further into hell.

OF MUSES

HOLLOW

I will stand here,
hollow,
empty hands
turned skyward.

I will stand here,
silent
or silenced.

Aching
for anything
but the sound
of wolves
howling
at broken skies,

Anything,
but the sound
of falling doves.

Anything
but this.
Seen by one
who could not love
and loved by those
who would not see.

OF ASHES

FIRE

I only ever let go of hope
when it tore the flesh from my palms,
or when I named it rage
and burned it to the ground.

OF MUSES

SOMETIMES

You loved me
as I loved you.

You loved me
with outstretched palms,
and silent nights,
and the distant thunder
of maybe.

You loved me
with ferocious frailty,
and hungry words.

You loved me
with tomorrows,
and the dreams
that grew in defiance
along the banks
of our sorrow.

You loved me
as I loved you.

Reluctantly.
And completely.
And only sometimes.

STORM

I could feel it sometimes.
The way goodbye
hung heavy
on the horizon.

The way the air
was thick
with silence.

The way I could smell the rain.

And I'd take cover,
and I'd wait.

I'd wait to begin again.

SALVATION

He looked at me as if
I could find salvation in him,
and he in me,
and part of me
wanted desperately
to believe.

I kissed him
with my poisoned lips,
and broke his heart
as an act
of mercy.

FREE

I loved him,
maybe more ferociously
than I had loved anyone,
or maybe
just enough
to keep him free
of me.

OF MUSES

BOUND

I was bound here,
mired in years
of whatever this wasn't,
terrified that I'd
not love like this again.
Or perhaps
I was terrified
that I would.

LESSON

The hardest lesson
I never learned
was how to turn my back
on what if.

OF MUSES

COLD

Ask not why I receive you
with cold eyes,
and icy hands.

Even the trees
shed their golden tears,
and stand,
frigid,
in silent defiance
of summer's betrayal.

BETRAYAL

Words are not required of deceit.
Your betrayal exists in your silence.

TRAGIC

Your love is the most tragic of all.

It's bleary-eyed questions,
and handwritten letters,
and words left unsaid.

It's gentle pauses at midnight
or watching the dawn.

It's reluctant daydreams,
and open palms, and open arms.

It's rainy days,
and Venice side-streets,
and cobblestone walkways
to anywhere but here.

OF ASHES

It's old stones, older tales,
and the tombs of the gods.

It's finding my feet,
and then running,
and learning to fly.

It's other loves, and other lives,
and roads we took in other times.

Your love is expansive.
and perfect,
and tragic,
and you never
really loved me
at all.

THIS HEART

I did not ask much
of you.
Or anyone.
Anyone.
Anyone.

I just asked
for someone
someone
anyone
that could replace
the cravings
or the addictions
or the drugs
that blacken these lungs
or this heart.
This heart.
This
fucking
heart.

Craving always,
to burn,
or fall silent.
Or asleep.
Or just
numb.

BURNED

I tasted the longing
on your lips.
The nostalgia.
I wondered
if you could
be brave enough
to claim me,
or if you would stand
on the bridge
as it burned.

RELIEF

But to weep.
I had forgotten how to weep.
I cried often enough;
sometimes, at old movies, or in empathy,
and once out of relief.

But to weep.
Ten thousand tears
behind glass,
behind pride,
behind fear
of falling alone.

And then you.
Weeping for us.
For me.
For what I couldn't say
even if I'd found words.

And I wept with you.
For us.
For me.
For what I couldn't say
even if I'd found words.

OF ASHES

LETTER BOXES

Empty letter boxes
on emptier side streets;
waiting
for letters
I haven't sent.

Sleeping scripted stories
of wishes and glories;
decaying,
and silent
in cardboard tombs.

Dusty proclamations
to yesterday's lovers;
discarded,
never reaching
empty letter boxes.

TOO MUCH

I had to go.
I always
had to go.

Perhaps I
didn't' t know
how to love you.

Or perhaps
it was fear.

Of being
too much.
And not
enough.

Or chaining
you to all
that I was.

And wasn't.

OF ASHES

MY NAME

I wanted to know
if my name
tasted like blood
as it rolled
off your tongue.

You asked me
why I was there,
as if I hadn't spent years
at your feet.

OF MUSES

INDIFFERENCE

I did not come here
for this.

I did not crawl
breathless
through other loves
in other lives
just to fall
or kneel
before the throne
of your ambivalence,
or to kiss the ring
of your indifference.

I did not gasp
through airless days
and week-long nights
to pledge fealty
to maybes
and somedays
or one days.

No.
I did not
come here
for this.

OF ASHES

GARDENS

When she goes,
she may cry,
but not for you.

She will grieve
for dreams unrealized,
weep for gardens
that never grew,
and for the home
she has yet to find.

ECHO

I was satisfied
to haunt your memories,
to carve my name
in your psyche,
to echo in hallways,
with shadows of maybes,
to whisper your name
in fragrant dreams,
and make your bones
ache for me.

MOSES

I finally knew
which of us
was the shore
and which
was the sea.

I'd spent years here,
Beckoned by you.
Crashing.
Retreating.
Capsizing,
leaving salty rivers
at your feet.

I parted for you
as if you could lead me
from some wilderness
into a promised land
that had never
been promised.

You may well be
the leader of men,
but you'd never again
command the sea.

OF MUSES

IRELAND

I will go,
where stormy seas
meet angry skies,
and cliffs are haunted
by lovers claimed
in years gone by.

I will go,
and I will pray
that those skies and that sea
have never heard your name.

ADDICTION

Not anymore.
Not again.

Bloodletting.
Or waiting.
Or believing
in fate.

I was stronger now.

I preferred
blistered feet
to track marks
these days.

OF MUSES

WRETCHED BONES

Take these wretched bones;
carve our names
where they speak of legends.

Take the breath
from my chest;
lay my weary soul beside you,
but promise to find me
forever in dreams.

OF ASHES

FADE

That's not what I meant
when I told you
I'd see you
in dreams.

I don't want to see
the light fade.
Or your heart stop.
Or mine break.

QUIET

Don't look at me
as if the beast in you
could quiet
the rage in me.

OF ASHES

BLEED

I touched your face,
and cut my palms
on your sharpened smile,
hoping to get you
from under my skin
if I let myself bleed.

DEMONS

We were not soul mates.
Our demons were.

CURSES

I hope you look for me
in every woman
that crosses
your path,
crosses your mind.

I hope you look for me
in restless dreams,
in old letters,
and foolish whims
of what could have been.

I hope you look for me
in photographs,
on winding roads,
and every place
that was ever filled
with my laughter.

I hope you find me sometimes,
on the curve of a neck,
in the swell of a breast,
in a peal of laughter
that evaporates
in a crowded room.

I hope you find me sometimes.
And I hope that when you find me,
you lose me all over again.

OF MUSES

ASH

And so I held
my love for you
in my mouth,
in my hands.

Flowing, falling,
over my tongue,
through my fingers,
like honey.
Like blood.

Molten.
Searing.
Ash.

And gone.

OF ASHES

HOME

All I ever wanted
was to come home
to a place
that couldn't
be taken
from me.

MILK-BREATH

Do you care to sit
and stay a while
and watch the decay
and decline
of a simpler time?

Come step outside and watch
through the window;
the air is cold
but the view is clearer out here.

Do you remember the days
when the milk-breath of babies
was calming, and soothing,
and all that we needed?

Do you remember the days
when the monsters would pause
and wait,
and we stood guard
over sleeping babes,
and their tiny lips
that would pucker
and pout
as they slept.

Those babies are bigger,
but they still stretch
with lanky limbs
in protest

against the dawn
and the monsters
that keep us awake.

Do you care to sit
and stay a while,
and dream with me
of a simpler time?

Do you remember
when we spoke so freely
of the milk-breath of babies,
when I trusted you to lead,
and you believed I would follow.

Soon to be strangers,
we no longer speak
of the milk-breath of babies.

We're just two people
who crave the same thing,
sitting silently,
with airless words
hanging in midair;
two people
planning other lives,
in secret,
out of fear of them.

MORNING

You loved me
for a moment
this morning.

Eyes danced
through deep laugh lines
and I remembered
how your laughter
tasted like mischief
and home.

I remembered what it was
to be loved by you.

Or at all.

I remembered
that we were strangers now,
but you loved
me for a moment
this morning.

OF ASHES

UNWRITTEN

I tried to write you a letter.

I would have carved
my soul into pages,
or confessed precious secrets
that have never
found their way
into words.

I would have shown you
the silent sorrow in me,
and the softness you spoke to
when you saved me
from the other side
of the world.

But pens turn to stone,
and pages to ash,
and airless words
fall in mid-flight.

OF MUSES

SLOW VIOLENCE

It's times like this
that I remember.
I remember
that naked souls
and outstretched palms
recoil at the
slow violence
of the dawn.

I remember
that I never really
had anywhere to fall,
and that longing
will always
long for you.

DIVORCE

All the things I never said
and never will
tumble from half-empty boxes
of what ifs and almosts.

Moments in time,
entombed or enshrined
in polaroid daydreams
and celluloid smiles.

Yellowed love letters
like wishes tied to branches,
mark the way back
to a home that just wasn't.

Sedated half-breaths.
Passing time.
Half awake.
Half alive.
Not existing in either.

So, I write until dawn,
with no reason to sleep,
or in fact, nor to wake.

Or to dream.
Or to want.
Or to say the things
I never said.

OF MUSES

THE ONE

She's laughter
in hollow hallways
and the ghost of what if.
She's windblown hair,
and torn blue jeans,
and torn palms.
She's lowered lashes
and eyes full of cut-and-run.
She's hands in your hair,
and pleading palms
pressed to your chest.
She's sleepy Sundays,
and old sweaters,
and bare feet in the rain.
She's old photographs,
and half written stories,
and roads almost taken.

She's the one.
And she's gone.

OF ASHES

ERODE

Will you think of me someday
on some distant shoreline?
Will you remember
how I was built to receive
the rising
and falling
of your tides?

Will you remember me someday
on some far-off horizon?
Will you recall
how you'd lap at my sharp edges
and pull away
when I started
to crumble?

And how you broke yourself
on me
and retreated
alone.

SHACKLED

We were strangers to the world,
both politely shackled
to a silence we didn't earn.

We never quite fit there,
or anywhere,
but we daydreamed
with clasped hands
about places and things
meant for anyone but us.

We scrubbed the age
from the old things
to mimic new things
that looked like aged things.

Sometimes we laughed like fools
through sunburnt smiles
and sometimes we made coffee.

We always made coffee.

We had wild ideas
and drove for miles,
or wrote manifestos
on a whim.

OF ASHES

Unspoken dialogues
and unneeded monologues
arranged themselves on our hearts
in a way that spelled 'courage',
and sometimes
we shouldered fear
for each other.

We sang sometimes,
or we raged
or we wept
or we danced
just for lack of a reason to stop.

We are strangers in the world now,
both politely shackled
to a silence
we certainly earned.

OF MUSES

GOLD

Branches stretched
to sparkling skies,
and fleeting clouds
held heavy sighs.
In autumnal glory
and bitter cold,
surely words
would have glittered gold.

GLANCE

Sometimes we'd cast a glance
over burdened shoulders
and heavy hearts.

We'd find sweetness there,
in the places between,
where sorrow and regret
trod heavy footprints
across the canvas
of what might have been.

And for a moment,
we'd dance again,
suspended in time,
to some old song
about seeing each
other in dreams.

TIDES

When the tides of yesterday
pull me under,
and the glow of the moon
feels too cold on my flesh,
when the dreams
of tomorrow
grow silent,
and the echoes
of all that should have been
begin to wail,
I look for you.

In that blackness,
I always look for you.

OF ASHES

UNIVERSE

And so I carved your name
in some corner of my psyche.
I swore solemn vows
to love you only in that place,
where today
slept at the feet
of tomorrow.

I spent days
practicing the art
of not loving you,
and counting down minutes
until I'd see you in dreams.

Days turned to nights,
into days,
into years,
and I loved you there only,
until the day that I couldn't.

And there you stood,
locking eyes with my demons
and the universe at your feet.

INSTINCT

There was always something
that made me look back,
some instinct
that demanded
I look
over my shoulder,
just in case
you could finally see me.

FLOORBOARDS

I wrapped myself
in my longing for you.

Cashmere lies and illusions,
pulled closer, tighter,
across lonely shoulders,
and I told myself
it was faith.

Bare feet
on old floorboards.

Slowly pacing,
retracing
haunted steps
that always lead
back to this place,
and the chill of knowing
you were gone.

WISHES

There are days sometimes,
when I remember.
I remember handfuls of bluebells
and roadside daisies,
and wishes that just might come true.

I remember freckled noses
and wide-eyed daydreams
of dancing in white dresses,
and I remember making plans
for days that never came.

There are days sometimes when I wish.
I wish that you'd asked me to dance,
or to laugh,
or to dream,
or to just to fall into you.

I wish you'd seen to my core,
that you'd spoken
to the softness in me,
and asked me to heal you.

I wish you'd asked me to rise.
To stand in my power,
for you, for us,
for freckled noses,
and daydreams
that crumbled
under fear and pride.

OF ASHES

I wish you'd asked me to trust you,
and then given me a reason to.
I wish you'd asked me to lean into you,
to take shelter,
to believe,
and have faith in you.

I wish you'd asked to know the dreamer,
the child,
the healer.

I wanted to sit
at the foot of your sorrow,
cleanse the weariness
from your soul
so you could see your own greatness.

I wish I could have made you strong.

More than anything,
I wish I could have been weak.

OF MUSES

LOST

I never lost love for you.
I lost hope.

SADDEST GRACE

Fleeting and in restless dreams
        sultry blues on ivory keys,
briefly, even rage and grief
        bowed their heads to listen.

Curse the dawn that begs me wake,
        turns blissful dark to wretched day,
and reverent hymn to saddest grace
        or forces me to miss him.

OF MUSES

WINDOW
I pretend sometimes that we've never met.

I pretend that we'd remained strangers in time,
that you had only smiled instead of saying hello,
and that you'd gone back to whatever
held your gaze out that window.

I pretend that I don't know what it's like
to be seen, to be known.
I pretend not to know
how your soul hungers for a love
you don't feel you deserve.

I pretend sometimes
that you can't read the space between lines
or the words I've never written
because I don't know what to say.

I pretend that you can't read the words on my heart
as if you had written them yourself,
and I pretend that the words
written on yours
aren't the same.

OF ASHES

I pretend that you don't control the tides
and your voice doesn't resonate
with a thunder that shakes my soul.

I pretend that there isn't a void
between your life and mine
and that things don't get lost somewhere
between all that is, and this.

I pretend sometimes that I've imagined it all,
and I don't know what it's like to dream,
or long, or to crave.

I pretend that I've created something
from nothing, just to believe in anything.

I pretend that maybe you'll smile at me
if I see you sitting by a window someday,
and we'll just be strangers in time.

MORE

Loving you
took everything I had.

Trying not to love you
took more.

YOURS

Beckoned back
into restless dreams,
where I can smell the salt on your skin,
and feel your hands in my hair.

You said "I miss you"
as if I was ever yours,
and I wanted
to sleep forever.

CHURCHES

We sat side by side,
in churches,
celebrating
the lives or the loves
of the people
we'd loved together.

We sat, politely,
as if there wasn't
a thirty-foot dead man
on the wall.
As if we hadn't
destroyed each other.

We sat worlds apart,
making small talk
about irises
or in silence.

And we returned
to the lives
we hated.

SOMEWHERE

Take me away from this place.
Take me
to where words don't hang airless
on heavy hearts,
where wishes
aren't silenced
by darkened yesterdays.

Take me somewhere
that resonates with your laughter.

Take me
where hope shimmers
in sparkling eyes
and where your hands
are warm
and holding mine.

OF MUSES

YOUR NAME

I wrote your name
ten thousand times.
Stitched into edges.
Scratched into margins.

I wrote your name
on wet windows
with wistful fingers,
on rainy days
when skies
hung heavy
and low.

I wrote your name
ten thousand times.
On skylines.
Or shorelines.

Or anytime
I needed
to leave part
of you
behind.

OF ASHES

AGAIN

If it cannot be
in this life,
I will love you
in the next.
I will carve my soul
into these pages,
like wishes
tied to branches,
and pray you might
find me there.
Perhaps we'll meet again,
over coffee,
and speak of poets
from days gone by.

OF MUSES

MUSES BURN

I laid my love
on the pyre
at the foot of madness,
where longing
only longed
for something to long for.

I fashioned freedom
from the flame,
and ink from the ash,
because even muses burn.

ABOUT THE AUTHOR

Mira Hadlow is an outspoken Canadian writer, an advocate, self-proclaimed romantic, and champion for the underdog. After an abusive relationship rendered her permanently deaf, she turned to writing as a path to healing and has become passionate about being a voice for the voiceless.

Mira believes in ferocious vulnerability, unapologetic truth, and bravely facing one's shadow side. She believes the path to healing is found by learning to sit with -and make room for- grief, fear, and sorrow.

She is a quirky, creative soul and you can usually find her renovating a kitchen, losing her cup of coffee for the forty seventh time, or picking a fight with an authority figure.

Made in United States
Orlando, FL
13 December 2021